Lucy The Cat Mystery Queen

Pertti Pietarinen

Library of Congress Control Number: 2020913808

ISBN: 979-8664533118 (Paperback)
ISBN: 978-9527304136 (eBook)

DEDICATION

This Book is dedicated to

Lucy The Cat

Read other books from Pertti Pietarinen

Lucy The Cat: ISBN 978-1494444136, 2014, http://www.amazon.com/dp/B00IARLDCY
God's Children: ISBN 978-1497567399, 2014, http://www.amazon.com/dp/B00JPT3L4O
Lucy The Cat: Little Brother: ISBN 978-1500770396, 2014, http://www.amazon.com/dp/B00MQI99N8
Lucy The Cat Play With Me: ISBN 978-1505607000, 2015, http://www.amazon.com/dp/B00STTT01Y
Lucy The Cat And Little Kittens: ISBN 978-1515385288, 2015, http://www.amazon.com/dp/B014FPTOM0
Lucy The Cat Christmas: ISBN 978-1517153700, 2015, https://www.amazon.com//dp/B0178BBRCS
Lucy The Cat Sushi Time: ISBN 978-1532867163, 2016, https://www.amazon.com/dp/B01FG17V4K
Lucy The Cat Beauty And The Feast: ISBN 978- 1539533993, 2017, https://www.amazon.com/dp/1539533999
Lucy The Cat In Tokyo: ISBN 978-1547269303, 2017 http://www.amazon.com/dp/1547269308
Lucy The Cat In Tokyo 2: ISBN 978-1977655752, 2018 http://www.amazon.com/dp/1977655750
Lucy The Cat Enchanted Forest: ISBN 978-1723700026, https://www.amazon.com/dp/1723700029

Books in Finnish and in Japanese

Kissa Kiiskinen sankarina ja muita satuja: ISBN 978-9522303141, Aurinko Kustannus Oy, 2014
Lucy-kissa, Lucy The Cat: ISBN 978-1497535633, 2014, http://www.amazon.com/dp/B00JPSSY2E,
Lucy-kissa ja pikkuveli: ISBN 978-1502764096, 2014, http://www.amazon.com/dp/B00OHDBYW4
Lucy-kissa leiki kanssani: ISBN 978-1507563403, 2015, http://www.amazon.com/dp/B00STZ3CRQ
Lucy-Kissa ja pikku sisarukset: ISBN 978-9523189782, 2015, http://www.amazon.com/dp/B015SRKNDS
Lucy-Kissan joulu: ISBN 978-9523189942, 2015 ISBN 978-1502399366, 2015, https://www.amazon.com/dp/B017DCXLKl
Lucy-Kissan Hurmaava Sushihetki: ISBN 978-9523309142, 2016, https://www.amazon.com/dp/9523309145

Lucy The Cat Bilingual Japanese – English, ISBN 978-1502399366, 2014
ねこのルーシー　バイリンガル　日本語 - 英語, https://www.amazon.com/dp/1502399369/
Lucy The Cat and Little Brother Bilingual Japanese – English, ISBN 978-1503085022, 2014
ねこのルーシー　と　ちいさな　おとうと　バイリンガル　日本語 - 英語, https://www.amazon.com/dp/1503085023/
Lucy The Cat Play With Me Bilingual Japanese – English, ISBN 978-1511672931, 2015
ねこのルーシー　わたしと　あそんで　バイリンガル　日本語 - 英語, https://www.amazon.com/dp/1511672935/
Lucy The Cat And Little Kittens Bilingual Japanese – English , ISBN 978-1517348137, 2015
ねこのルーシーと　ちいさな　こねこたち　バイリンガル：日本語 ー 英語, http://www.amazon.com/dp/1517348137
Lucy The Cat Christmas Bilingual Japanese – English ISBN 978-1517754747, 2015
ねこのルーシー　クリスマス　バイリンガル：日本語 ー 英語, http://www.amazon.com/dp/1517754747
Lucy The Cat Sushi Time Bilingual Japanese – English, ISBN 978-1533246226, 2016
ねこのルーシー　おすしの　じかん　バイリンガル：日本語 - 英語, https://www.amazon.com/dp/153324622X
Lucy The Cat Beauty And The Feast Bilingual Japanese – English, ISBN 978- 1545540862, 2017
ねこのルーシー　び　と　よろこび　バイリンガル：日本語 - 英語, https://www.amazon.com/dp/1545540861
Lucy The Cat in Tokyo Bilingual Japanese – English, ISBN 978- 1545540862, 2017
ねこのルーシー　とうきょうへ　いく　バイリンガル：日本語 - 英語, https://www.amazon.com/dp/1974145352
Lucy The Cat in Tokyo 2 Bilingual Japanese – English, ISBN 978-1986820462, 2018
ねこのルーシー　とうきょうへ　いく　2　バイリンガル：日本語 - 英語, https://www.amazon.com/dp/1986820467
Lucy The Cat Enchanted Forest Bilingual Japenese – English, ISBN 978-1726817585, 2018
ねこのルーシー　まほうの　もり　バイリンガル：日本語 - 英語, https://www.amazon.com/dp/172681758X

Learn more about Lucy The Cat, other books and new releases:
http://www.pietarinen.org
https://www.facebook.com/lucythecat
https://www.facebook.com/GodsChildrenBook

My last night was filled with sweet and beautiful dreams. I was sleeping like a log. Oh boy, I slept really well! I woke up early in the morning and felt really refreshed. I was ready for new adventures. I did not know what would wait for me. I felt very excited.

Anyway, I ate a tasty breakfast, tuna and shrimps, my favorite food. My human mom knows what I can not resist. Once I saw a photo of a huge tuna. I think it weighted over 200 kilos. Hope I could catch one of those and I would have my favorite breakfast and lunch and dinner forever.

Before you leave your safe home and your mom and dad you need to be well prepared. You never know who you meet and what happens. You don't know if you meet the good, the bad or the ugly. You have to keep your eyes open. Therefore, I had to sharpen my nails. They had to be razor sharp. On my journey I would be on my own and nobody else would defend me. Safety first!

I stepped out and closed the front door carefully. My human mom and dad were not at home, so I had to take care of the closing of the door. I started to walk down the empty street. I felt so happy.

Behind the corner I met my best friend, the good fairy. I told her that I was prepared to travel and wanted to enjoy a good adventure. She smiled to me and promised to help me. The wind started to blow gently and - wow! I was flying over the street and fields and forests. Here we go!

Suddenly I was in front of an ancient building. It looked like a Mayan temple. It was really fascinating and magnificent. When I admired it, something miraculous happened. There were like horns growing on the top of the temple.

I felt like a wind blowing and in the next moment, a human, a lady, dropped down from somewhere. She was smiling friendly and asked my name. I told that I am Lucy The Cat. She said: "Nice to meet you! My name is Joy. Welcome to Chichen itza, Mayan temple and the Palace of Mystery Queen. People are not allowed to enter inside the palace. But, because you are a cat, you can join me and come in. Let's go." I was a little afraid, but I followed her.

"Who is Mystery Queen", I wondered.

"You will understand, when you see her" Joy answered.

Together we went behind the temple. There we found a secret door and passage. I felt excited. Then there were stairs going down. Stairs looked slippery and we had to walk very carefully. I started to feel afraid. The stairs went down, down down…

Next, I saw an old troubadour playing his lute. I think he was playing some cat's polka tune. His big, black cat was singing when troubadour was playing.

The troubadour welcomed me and asked to continue to the Mystery Queen's palace.

This was very exciting. We continued deeper into the cave.

Next room looked scary. There were snakes everywhere slowly moving and crawling. A beautiful parrot was shouting: "Don't come here. This is our world. Beat it!"

Then I heard a thunderous sound, and someone was flying around us and when it landed, I realized that it was an angry looking dragon. I was shocked and started to tremble. Joy was standing by my side and told the creatures to calm down and let us go further.

Luckily, we were allowed to continue to the next room. But it was at least as scary. Full of skeletons and skulls piled up. I think I saw some treasures, too. Maybe diamonds and gold coins like in pirates' hiding places. And snakes and lizards were guarding the treasures.

There was also some strange writing on the wall. Maybe the letters were from some ancient culture. I did not understand anything. Joy whispered: "Don't be afraid, we must continue, if you want to meet the Queen."

When I opened the next door and entered in the new room, I knew, it was a wrong decision to follow Joy. There was a small room, like a prison cell and a mean looking guy was guarding at the door.

"Well, well, well, who came in? Who are you?" the guy snarled in a creaking voice. "We don't want to have any spies here. You will never get out of here. I will lock you in this barren cell ha, ha, ha…"

There I was standing like frozen and I could not take a single step. The ugly guy locked me in the cell, and I was left alone. There was only a small desk and an empty bowl on the desk.

I was sad and wanted to cry. Why did I leave home to search adventures? Can I ever return home? I decided to lay down on the floor and wait if someone brings food and something to drink. I really missed my tuna and shrimp.

After a while I realized that there was a window in my prison cell. Beautiful light came through the window. Sun rays were dancing in my room. I wanted to see what was behind the window. How can I climb so high? Can I jump high enough?

I concentrated with my all mental power and jumped as high I could. Luckily, I reached the windowsill, but bars covered the window and there was no way out. Anyway, it was refreshing to see sunshine and the empty backyard.

Beautiful butterflies came flying to comfort me in my misery. They were flying and dancing like bringing news from the free world. I started to feel better and fell in sleep on the windowsill.

Then I heard someone coming to the door. I woke up and Joy was on the door with the troubadour. She was smiling when she unlocked the door.

"Please follow me, you are free" Joy said. "You endured all the tests and can now meet our mighty queen."

The troubadour started to play his lute and together we marched out of the cell to the castle courtyard. Some miracles happened and I saw my own face in the middle of the flower petals.

Joy led us into the castle. Mystery Queen was already waiting for me.

When I saw the queen, I understood why her name was Mystery Queen. Joy whispered to me, that no-one is allowed to see the queen's face.

I felt very happy and humble. I knew that the royal protocol required me to bow. So, I did.

The queen was friendly, and we enjoyed the afternoon tea together. Actually, I don't like so much tea. But I wanted to be kind and polite. The queen understood that the tea is not for me, so she asked to bring a bowl of shrimps and another bowl full of cream. What a feast!

The queen was busy, and she had to leave me and return to her office. She asked Joy and the troubadour to arrange a special program for me before I would return home.

I was guided to the top of the Chichen itza temple, where visitors are not allowed to go. It was charming to be up there and enjoy the magnificent view. I felt so special and happy. I think I was growing bigger and bigger, at least hundred times to my normal size.

The sunshine was very hot, and I started to feel tired. I asked Joy, if I can go home. But then I was wondering, how can I return home. Joy started laugh and explained that their queen is very modern, and their kingdom is very advanced.

Joy took me down from the temple top and led me to the secret part of the courtyard. There was a huge rocket ready to go and Joy guided me into the rocket and promised that in a few seconds I will be at home.

Before going in I noticed that they had even painted my name on the rocket.

Have you ever had your name painted on the rocket?

In a moment I was sitting inside the capsule of the rocket. Thundering sound from the rocket engines started to roar and, in a few seconds, I was on my way. Fire and smoke almost covered the castle.

I landed back home before I noticed anything. Home sweet home.

Happy to be back at home again. It was fun but just now I don't want to meet any queens or kings. At least not today. Maybe tomorrow a new adventure is waiting. But now I want to jump to dad's lap.

Made in the USA
Middletown, DE
20 September 2020